martinis

martinis

ben reed

photography by william lingwood

RYLAND
PETERS
& SMALL
LONDON NEW YORK

Senior Designers Paul Tilby
and Susan Downing
Editor Miriam Hyslop
Production Controller Gavin Bradshaw

Art Director Gabriella Le Grazie
Publishing Director Alison Starling

Mixologist Ben Reed
Stylist Helen Trent

First published in the United States in 2005
by Ryland Peters & Small, Inc.,
519 Broadway
5th Floor
New York, NY 10012
www.rylandpeters.com

10 9 8 7 6 5 4 3 2 1

Text © Ben Reed 2005

Design and photographs
© Ryland Peters & Small 2005

Printed in China.

ISBN 1 84597 162 0

Library of Congress Cataloging-in-
Publication-Data is available on request.

contents

introduction

What is a martini? To many drinkers it can only be one thing: gin and vermouth with either a lemon zest or olive garnish. If this were the case and the boundaries for producing a martini were this rigid, we would not have the variety of "martinis" that we enjoy today.

The argument of how best to make a martini is an outdated one. There are any number of ways to make a classic martini—all depend on personal taste (and how can that be a bad thing?). The trend of calling any drink prepared using gin or vodka as a base and served in a martini cocktail glass a "martini" is, I think, what infuriates the purists. Just between you and me, I take secret pleasure in defying these sticklers for tradition. Indeed, I go so far as to pounce on such dinosaurs with a war cry of "try a Cheesecake Martini on for size!"—less to influence opinion than to check that they are still awake!

I've categorized these drinks into groups to give you an idea of the differences in the ways they are made. Some require a little bit of preparation, others rely on the freshest, ripest fruit; for others still, the most delicate touch of an added ingredient is what lends the drink its individuality.

Taking ideas from cocktail bars around the world, along with a healthy smattering of my own creations, I've put together a list of martinis that should delight and amaze but, most important, add a little color to the cheeks! You'll find that it's a wide-ranging collection—some you will love, some you may hate, but that's the whole fun of cocktails. There's a cocktail for everyone, and once you find it, you're well on the way to a drop of enlightenment.

techniques

The three basic methods used to make a martini are stirring, shaking, and pouring (also called the diamond method). Each method, performed correctly, has a direct effect on the character of the drink and the way it appears in the glass.

STIRRING

Place a barspoon into a mixing glass and fill it with ice. Stir gently in a continuous motion until the glass is cold to the touch. Add a dash of vermouth and stir (each stir should last for about 10 revolutions—try to avoid chipping the ice, which dilutes the martini) before discarding the dilution and the vermouth. Finally, add the liquor and stir.

SHAKING

Add the ingredients to a shaker and fill it with ice. Shake with strong, sharp movements (remembering to keep a hand on both parts of the shaker!). This method is useful when you mix creamy martinis.

POURING (or diamond method)

For the coldest, purest martini—simply place a bottle of gin or vodka and your martini glasses in a freezer for 6 hours. To serve, add a dash of vermouth to a chilled glass, swill it around, and discard. Pour the frozen liquor into the glass for an unadulterated cocktail.

equipment

For a "stirred" martini you will need a **mixing glass** with a **strainer**. A **cocktail shaker** is essential for those who prefer their martinis "shaken." One with a lid and a strainer is ideal. You will also need a **jigger**. Modern jiggers are the most useful as they measure both 1 oz. and 2 oz. (a double and a single measure). A long-handled **barspoon** is useful for stirring drinks and "muddling" or crushing fruit, herbs, etc.

garnishes

The traditional garnishes for a martini are of course an **olive** or a **lemon twist**. A certain amount of poetic license can be used when creating garnishes for newer cocktails. Your choice of garnish should complement both the taste and the appearance of the drink. A **lemon zest** (or **twist**), properly prepared and added to the surface of a classic martini, transforms the drink. Take a sharp knife and gently skim a length of peel from the lemon—the zest should be fine with no pith. Squeeze the zest over the drink, wipe it around the rim, and then drop it into the liquid. Another type of lemon garnish is the **lemon peel**—simply slice a thin peel from a lemon and drop it into the drink. For a **flaming orange zest**, take a thick orange zest and squeeze it, skin down, over a flame and the surface of the drink (the juice from citrus fruit is flammable); then drop the zest into the martini. Another simple and effective way to garnish your martini is to **"rim"** the glass with cocoa powder, salt, or nutmeg. To do this, wipe a piece of orange around the rim of the glass and place the glass rim down in the powder, creating a neat rim around the edge. Make sure the powder does not mix directly with the martini.

classic

As any mixologist worth his salt will tell you, there's very little point in experimenting with modern cocktail variations unless you know your classics. The recipe for the classic martini, despite being strictly adhered to in certain circles, is also one of the most dabbled-with recipes in the history of the cocktail. The classic martini has evolved, in keeping with social tastes, into the ultra-cold, ultra-dry, predominantly vodka-based cocktail enjoyed today.

classic martini

This is how I would make a "standard martini" for anyone who asked for one. While the pouring or diamond method (see page 9) is faster and the resultant drink stronger (less diluted), stirring the cocktail is a more authentic method and the original labor of love for any bartender.

**a dash of vermouth
(Noilly Prat or Martini Extra Dry)**
2 oz. chilled gin or vodka
an olive or a lemon twist, to garnish

Add both the Ingredients to a mixing glass filled with ice and stir. Strain into a frosted martini glass and garnish with an olive or a twist. Alternately use the diamond technique.

gibson

The leading theory behind the origin of this classic martini is that it was first made at the beginning of the 20th century for Charles Gibson, a famous illustrator, at the Players Club in New York. Whatever its roots, this classic drink has truly withstood the test of time.

Add both the ingredients to a mixing glass filled with ice and stir. Strain into a frosted martini glass and garnish with a cocktail onion.

a dash of vermouth (Noilly Prat or Martini Extra Dry)

2 oz. chilled gin or vodka

a cocktail onion, to garnish

gimlet

A great litmus test for a bar's cocktail capability
—too much lime and the drink turns sickly, not
enough and the drink is too strong. This one needs to
be shaken hard to guarantee a sharp freezing zestiness.

Add both the ingredients to a shaker
filled with ice, shake hard and strain
into a frosted martini glass.

1 oz. Rose's lime cordial
1¾ oz. gin or vodka

dirty

This martini is also known as the FDR, after the man who
called an end to Prohibition in the '30s. Fittingly, the great
president was an accomplished bartender who loved nothing
more than flourishing his shaker for any head of state with
a like mind or a dry palate.

a dash of vermouth (Noilly Prat or Martini Extra Dry)
2 oz. chilled gin or vodka
a large dash of brine from the olive or onion jar
an olive, a twist of lemon, or a cocktail onion, to garnish

Add all the ingredients to a shaker filled with
ice, shake sharply, and strain into a frosted
martini glass. Garnish with an olive, a twist
of lemon, or a cocktail onion.

white lady

2 oz. London Dry gin
¾ oz. Cointreau
¾ oz. fresh lemon juice
½ egg white

Invented by legendary mixologist, Harry McElhone at Harry's New York Bar in Paris, the White Lady was originally made with crème de menthe instead of gin.

Add all ingredients to a shaker filled with ice, shake vigorously and strain into a frosted martini glass.

vesper

Christened by James Bond in the film *Casino Royale*—Bond named the drink after his Bond girl de-jour Vesper Lynd. A shaken, medium-dry concoction.

Add all the ingredients to a shaker filled with ice, shake, and strain into a frosted martini glass. Garnish with the lemon peel and serve.

1½ oz. gin

½ oz. vodka

¼ oz. Kina Lillet (French vermouth)

a long lemon peel, to garnish

montgomery

1 part vermouth
15 parts gin or vodka
**an olive or a lemon zest,
to garnish**

This martini is named after Field Marshall
Montgomery, an Allied hero of World War II.
Considering "Monty" fought in the North African
desert, it's surprising that he didn't prefer
something less dry!

Stir all the ingredients in a mixing glass filled with
ice and strain into a frosted martini glass. Garnish
with an olive or lemon zest.

horse's

½ oz. ginger liqueur
2 oz. vodka
a whole lemon peel,
to garnish

This recipe stems from the days when gin and vodka were considered medicinal. The ginger would have been added not only to flavor the elixir, but also to act as an herbal remedy to cure most ills.

Add both ingredients to a shaker filled with ice, shake sharply, and strain into a frosted martini glass. Garnish with a whole lemon peel.

martinez

2 oz. Old Tom Gin

½ oz. sweet vermouth

a dash of orange bitters

a large dash of maraschino

a lemon twist, to garnish

The Martinez is believed to be the first documented martini, dating back as far as 1849, when it was mixed for a miner who had just struck gold in the town of Martinez, California. Its sweet flavors were geared to appeal to the taste buds of the time and the availability of certain liquors.

Add all the ingredients to a shaker filled with ice, shake, and strain into a frosted martini glass. Garnish with a lemon twist.

essentially vox

2 oz. Vox vodka

a large dash of vermouth

lemon, lime, and orange zests, to garnish

On occasion a new way of dressing a martini is called for. By bottom zesting your martini with the lemon, lime, and orange zest the citrus flavors will carry through the cocktail.

Take thin zests of lemon, lime, and orange, twist them together and drop into the bottom of an empty pre-chilled martini glass. Stir all ingredients over ice and strain into the martini glass.

personaltini

As a lover of martinis of all shapes and sizes, I didn't find it easy to name my favorite, but here it is. A naked black Stoli martini, stirred and served up. Create and name your own martini.

2 oz. Stolichnaya vodka
a black olive, to garnish

Add the Stoli vodka to a mixing glass filled with ice, stir until the mixing glass frosts, and strain into a frosted martini glass. Garnish with a black olive.

smokey martini

Try using a really smokey Isla malt as the modifying flavoring for this cocktail. True to making any martini, the key to this drink is to make it as cold as possible.

2 oz. gin

¼ oz. dry vermouth

½ oz. whiskey

Add the gin, a dash of dry vermouth, and the whiskey to a shaker filled with cracked ice. Shake sharply and strain into a frosted martini glass.

aviation
cocktail

This classic cocktail has been hidden away in the archives for too long. Dust it down and enjoy its delights.

2 oz. London dry gin

1 oz. fresh lemon juice

½ oz. Maraschino liqueur

Shake all ingredients hard over cubed ice, strain into a frosted martini glass.

adonis

2½ oz. Fino sherry
1 oz. Cinzano Rosso vermouth
4 drops orange bitters
orange twist, to garnish

This delicate, aromatic aperitif is thought to have been invented two centuries ago.

Stir all ingredients in a mixing glass filled with ice. Strain into a frosted martini glass and garnish with a thin orange twist.

opal martini

2 oz. gin
1 oz. Cointreau
1½ oz. fresh orange juice
orange zest, to garnish

Experiment with different gins to create the perfect balance. There are so many great and varied gins on the market today, you can almost create a new drink each time.

Add all ingredients to a shaker filled with ice, shake sharply, and strain into a pre-chilled martini glass. Garnish with an orange zest.

the ultimate

Every martini should be made using the very finest components. Make this martini the "ultimate" by choosing from the exceptional quality alcohol now available.

1 drop Vya dry vermouth

2 oz. chilled ultra-premium gin or vodka

a twist of lemon or an olive, to garnish

Rinse a frosted martini glass with the vermouth and discard. Add the liquor and garnish with a twist of lemon or an olive.

manhattan

The Manhattan is the un-identical twin of the martini and for that it deserves a mention. Replace your white liquor (gin or vodka) with a dark spirit (American whiskey) and substitute the dry vermouth with sweet. Instead of garnishing with an olive, use a cherry.

2 oz. bourbon
½ oz. sweet vermouth
cherry, to garnish

Add the ingredients to a mixing glass filled with ice (first ensure all the ingredients are very cold), and stir the mixture until chilled. Strain into a frosted martini glass, add the garnish, and serve.

bronx

Created at the Waldorf Astoria in New York by head bartender Johnnie Salon.

2 oz. gin
1 oz. fresh orange juice
¼ oz. sweet vermouth
¼ oz. dry vermouth
orange zest, to garnish

Add all ingredients to a shaker filled with ice, shake sharply, and strain into a pre-chilled martini glass. Garnish with an orange zest.

fresh + fruity

The fresh and fruity martini started as a back-lash against the prevalent cocktail movement of the '80s—that of sticking a chocolate bar into a bottle of vodka for a few weeks and trying to drink the resultant sludge. Rather than rely on various drinks manufacturers to create credible fruit-flavored vodkas, we (the cocktail cognoscenti) decided to regulate the flavors and the concentration of our own martinis. By simply macerating the freshest, ripest fruit with vodka or gin in a shaker, you, too, can create an irresistible martini.

pomegranate

Because this is one of the subtler
of the fruit martinis, you must make
sure the pomegranate is ripe. Try
to avoid getting any of the fruit's
bitter pith in the drink, as this would
destroy its delicate balance.

2 oz. vodka

½ pomegranate
   or ½ oz. pomegranate juice

a dash of simple syrup

pomegranate seeds, to garnish

Spoon the pomegranate "flesh" into
a shaker and crush, using a muddler
or the flat end of a barspoon. Add
ice to the shaker with the remaining
ingredients. Shake sharply and strain
into a frosted martini glass. Garnish
with a few pomegranate seeds.

cherry

3 stoned fresh cherries
2 oz. vodka
1 oz. thick cherry juice
a dash of cherry schnapps

This martini can also be made using the juice from canned cherries—it may not sound as nice but wait until you taste it.

Crush the cherries in a shaker. Add ice and the remaining ingredients, shake sharply, and strain into a frosted martini glass.

pear

2 oz. vodka

½ oz. Poire Williams eau de vie

a thin pear slice, to garnish

This fruit martini is certainly not for the faint-hearted. Unlike a lot of the fruit martinis, whose sweetness belies their strength, this one pulls no punches.

Shake all the ingredients in a shaker filled with ice and strain into a frosted martini glass. Garnish with a thin slice of pear and serve.

raspberry

2 oz. vodka

a dash of framboise

a dash of orange bitters

1 oz. raspberry purée

2 fresh raspberries, to garnish

The Raspberry is an old favorite of mine. This martini should be fairly thick in consistency, so if you aren't using purée, use a handful of raspberries to make sure it flows down your throat like molasses.

Shake all the ingredients in a shaker filled with ice and strain into a frosted martini glass. Garnish with two fresh raspberries.

lychee martini

Considering how easy this is to make and devilishly difficult to resist, I'm surprised this cocktail isn't a world favorite. Keep it simple for best effect.

2 oz. vodka

1 oz. lychee syrup (from a can of lychees)

a dash of simple syrup

1 lychee, to garnish

Add all ingredients into a shaker filled with ice, shake and strain into a pre-chilled martini glass. Garnish with a canned lychee.

fresca

The Fresca was invented to be served long with lemonade as a refreshing summer drink, but for every drinker who wants their thirst quenched, there will always be two who want their socks knocked off—and who am I to argue? See opposite for a choice of ingredients.

Add the ingredients to a shaker filled with ice, shake sharply, and strain into a frosted martini glass. Garnish and serve.

basil and honey fresca

2 oz. vodka

a dash of lime juice

a dash of grapefruit juice

2 sprigs of basil, crushed

a teaspoon of honey

a basil leaf, to garnish

orange and pear fresca

2 oz. vodka

a dash of lime juice

a dash of grapefruit juice

a slice of orange, crushed

a slice of pear, crushed

a dash of simple syrup

an orange zest, to garnish

port and blackberry fresca

2 oz. vodka

½ oz. port

a dash of lime juice

a dash of grapefruit juice

6 blackberries (two to garnish)

french

The French martini is great for parties since it is light and creamy, and simple to make in bulk. Shake this one hard when preparing it, and you will be rewarded with a thick white froth on the surface of the drink.

2 oz. vodka

a large dash of Chambord (or crème de mure)

3 oz. fresh pineapple juice

Add all the ingredients to a shaker filled with ice, shake sharply, and strain into a frosted martini glass.

citrus

2 oz. Cytryonowka vodka
1 oz. lemon juice
1 oz. Cointreau
a dash of simple syrup
a lemon zest, to garnish

Another old favorite, the citrus needs to be shaken hard to take the edge off the lemon. Try substituting lime for lemon for a slightly more tart variation.

Add all the ingredients to a shaker filled with ice, shake sharply, and strain into a frosted martini glass. Garnish with the lemon zest.

red snapper

The Red Snapper was the name given to the Bloody Mary in the 1940s when the original name was deemed too risqué for American sensibilities at the St. Regis Hotel in New York. We've taken the name and changed the format—make sure this one is extra spicy.

2 oz. Old Tom gin

3 oz. tomato juice

SPICE MIX:

4 dashes of Tabasco

a pinch of celery salt

2 dashes of lemon juice

a pinch of ground black pepper

4 dashes Worcestershire sauce

black pepper or lemon zest, to garnish

Add all the ingredients to a shaker filled with ice, shake sharply, and strain into a frosted martini glass. Garnish with a sprinkle of black pepper or a lemon zest.

gazpacho

This savory drink might sound like a strange choice, but, trust me, it works! The Gazpacho came about when a friend and I went out for brunch and were looking for a change of drink from the Bloody Mary. Gazpacho was on the menu, so we put two and two together—et voila!

2 oz. pepper vodka

black pepper

1 cup gazpacho soup

chopped herbs, to garnish

Shake all the ingredients really hard with ice and strain into a martini glass. Sprinkle on some chopped herbs to garnish.

double vision

One of the first new batch of flavored vodka cocktails. This one can also be served long.

1 oz. Absolut Citron vodka
1 oz. Absolut Kurrant vodka
2 oz. cloudy apple juice
a dash Angostura bitters
a dash of lime cordial

Add all ingredients to a shaker filled with ice, shake sharply, and strain into a pre-chilled martini glass.

strawberry

Use the ripest strawberries in this martini. The strawberry flavor is enhanced by a dash of fraise de bois (strawberry liqueur), but it should be kept to a minimum compared to the amount of fresh strawberries.

Place the strawberries in a shaker and muddle with the flat end of a barspoon. Add the remaining ingredients, shake hard, and strain into a frosted martini glass.

3 fresh large strawberries

2 teaspoons simple syrup

2 oz. vodka

a large dash of fraise de bois

basil grande

4 strawberries
(one to garnish)

2 basil leaves
(one to garnish)

2 oz. Grand Marnier

1½ oz. Chambord
(or crème de mure)

3 oz. cranberry juice

One of the few martinis that doesn't contain vodka as a base. Expect lots of strong flavors in this extravagantly fruity concoction. It's a great alternative to creamy cocktails after dinner.

Crush the strawberries and the basil leaf in a shaker. Add the remaining ingredients with ice, shake sharply, and strain into a large frosted martini glass. Garnish with a strawberry and a basil leaf.

peach martini

It is well worth the effort of finding the unusual ingredients for this martini—try it and you'll agree that crème de pêche and peach bitters definitely bring something to the table.

2 oz. vodka

½ oz. crème de pêche

¼ oz. peach purée

2 dashes peach bitters

Add all ingredients to a shaker filled with ice, shake, and strain into a pre-chilled martini glass.

apple martini

This cocktail has been a staple
requirement for any cocktail bar in
America for a decade. Here's one
with a slight European twist to it.

Add all ingredients to a shaker filled
with ice, shake sharply and strain
into a pre-chilled martini glass.
Garnish with an apple fan, if you
have the patience!

2 oz. vodka

½ granny smith apple, muddled

¼ oz. Brentzen apple liqueur

½ oz. cloudy English apple juice

apple, to garnish

vine wine martini

Who says you shouldn't mix grape and grain?
An ultra-distilled vodka is preferred in this recipe
mixed with a nice Pinot Noir. Experiment with
the amount of simple syrup used and the type
of red wine.

2 oz. Vox vodka
1 oz. red wine
6 red grapes
a dash of simple syrup

Muddle the grapes in a mixing glass, add the
remaining ingredients, ice and shake. Strain into
a pre-chilled martini glass.

melon martini

This fruity martini went down a storm on a recent trip I made to America to commemorate the art of garnishing cocktails.

Shake all ingredients hard over ice and strain into a pre-chilled martini glass. Garnish with the melon balls and pineapple leaves.

2 oz. vodka

½ oz. melon liqueur

1 oz. fresh pineapple juice

a dash of lemon juice

melon balls (honeydew, cantaloupe, or watermelon), to garnish

pineapple leaves, to garnish

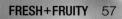

pontberry

The Pontberry martini is a snip to prepare since it involves no fresh fruit. Strong and sweet, it should appeal to a wide range of palates.

2 oz. vodka

3 oz. cranberry juice

a large dash of crème de mure

Shake all the ingredients in a shaker filled with ice. Strain into a frosted martini glass and serve.

blood martini

A bittersweet concoction that needs to be delicately balanced. The lime and the Campari provide the bitterness, while the sweet element comes in the form of the raspberry liqueur. Taste the drink before and after adding the orange zest—what a difference!

2 oz. vodka

½ oz. Campari

¼ oz. framboise

¼ oz. fresh lime juice

1 oz. cranberry juice

a dash of Cointreau

a flaming orange zest, to garnish

Add all the ingredients to a shaker filled with ice, shake sharply, and strain into a frosted martini glass. Garnish with a flaming orange zest.

absolutely fabulous

A cocktail with real sophistication and class—just the sort
of drink you can imagine the most faboulous people drinking!

1 oz. Stolichnaya vodka
½ oz. fraise de bois liqueur
1 oz. cranberry juice
champagne, to top up
strawberry, to garnish

Add all but the champagne to a shaker filled
with ice. Shake sharply and strain into
a pre-chilled martini glass. Garnish with
half a strawberry.

gotham

As sinister and mysterious as the name suggests. Try varying the amount of black Sambuca (one of the most underused cocktail ingredients I know) for a darker, more threatening result.

2½ oz. frozen Stolichnaya vodka

a dash of black Sambuca

Pour the vodka into a frosted martini glass, gently add the Sambuca, and serve.

clean+serene

"Clean and serene" martinis are designed for those of us who still enjoy the clarity and the purity of the classic, but appreciate an added touch of spice. They smooth and caress the taste buds with the same poetry of the originals, while delighting the senses with a hint of something extra. From the Thunderer with its perfumed touch of lavender, to the Gotham and its subtle traces of aniseed, these cocktails convey the elegance and sophistication of the classic martini with the added allure of extra taste.

thunderer

This cocktail smells almost perfumed. A hint of Parfait Amour— a beautifully named orange curaçao flavored with violets —and a tease of cassis is all this drink needs to achieve its flowery, distinctive taste.

Pour the Parfait Amour and cassis into a frosted martini glass. Add the frozen vodka and garnish with two blueberries.

2 oz. frozen vodka

2 drops of Parfait Amour

2 drops of cassis

2 blueberries, to garnish

applejack

1 oz. vodka

1 oz. Manzana apple liqueur

1 scant oz. Calvados

a thin slice of apple, to garnish

Taken from recipes using American apple brandy, this concoction relies heavily on the addition of Manzana apple liqueur, a green apple liqueur that lends a bitter-sweet quality to the martini.

Add all the ingredients to a mixing glass filled with ice, stir until the glass appears frosted, and strain into a frosted martini glass. Garnish with a thin slice of apple.

miller's martini

Created specifically to complement Miller's gin
by Alex Kammerling of IPBartenders.

2 oz. Miller's gin

¼ oz. elderflower cordial

lemon zest, to garnish

Rinse a pre-chilled martini glass with chilled
elderflower cordial. Stir the Miller's over ice and pour
into the martini glass. Garnish with a lemon zest.

CLEAN+SERENE

joe average

Despite its name, there is nothing average about this drink. Nor should the Pimm's in the recipe fool you—this is not a drink to be taken lightly!

2 oz. Stolichnaya vodka

¼ oz. Pimm's No. 1 cup liqueur

a thin slice of cucumber and a lemon zest, to garnish

Add the ingredients to a mixing glass filled with ice, stir until the glass appears frosted, and strain into a frosted martini glass. Garnish with a thin slice of cucumber and a lemon zest.

legend

Invented in London in the late '80s, this recipe has to be followed closely because too much of any of the ingredients can result in an unpalatable cocktail. Make sure you taste each concoction before you serve it.

2 oz. vodka
½ oz. crème de mure
½ oz. fresh lime juice
a dash of simple syrup

Add all the ingredients to a shaker filled with ice, shake sharply, and strain into a frosted martini glass.

decadent

To the old-fashioned martini drinker, there is no time or place for the more elaborate new concoctions. Yet with a martini—as with anything important in life—I believe there's room for a little poetic license. If the drink tastes amazing and maintains the level of elegance expected from a martini, then as far as I'm concerned, there's not a problem!

orange brûlée

The Orange Brûlée is a dessert drink that should be savored. You'll notice I don't recommend the caramelization process—would you trust a bartender with a blowtorch?

1 oz. Grand Marnier
1 oz. Amaretto
a dash of white crème de cacao
whipping cream, to top
thin strips of orange zest, to garnish

Add all the ingredients except the cream to a shaker filled with ice, shake sharply, and strain into a martini glass. Whip the cream and dollop it gently onto the surface of the drink. Crisscross with orange zest.

claret cobbler

The cobbler has long proven to be a classic that can take whatever time throws at it. The combination of fresh citrus juices, raspberry liqueur, and port or claret* may even have the wine buffs sitting up and paying attention …

one lemon slice
one lime wedge
one orange wheel
2 tablespoons claret or port
1 oz. vodka
1 oz. framboise

Muddle the fruit in a shaker. Add the remaining ingredients, shake sharply and strain into a frosted martini glass.
* *Red Bordeaux or Cabernet-Merlot blends.*

black bird

The Black Bird isn't a spur-of-the-moment type of drink. The work put in beforehand is in equal proportion to the look of amazement on its drinker's face. The Cointreau and the brandy in the mix draw all the juices out of the berries, and they combine with the alcohol in a most un-alcoholic way. One to be wary of.

1 oz. lemon juice

2 oz. lemon vodka

4 teaspoons Cointreau berry mix*

    ½ cup strawberries

    ½ cup raspberries

    ½ cup blueberries

    ½ cup cranberries

    1 oz. brandy

    1 oz. Cointreau

    1 lb superfine sugar

Place a scoop of berry mix into a frosted martini glass and press down. Pour the remaining ingredients into a shaker filled with ice, shake sharply, and gently strain the mixture into the martini glass.

* To make the berry mix, add all the ingredients to a container, stir once, and leave overnight. Stir once more before serving.

hazelnut

2 oz. vodka

¾ oz. crème de cacao (light)

¼ oz. Frangelico (hazelnut liqueur)

nutmeg powder (for the rim)

This martini has proven popular with men and women alike. A strong, clear chocolate martini with an undercurrent of hazelnut, perfect for after dinner with coffee—dessert and a nightcap rolled into one.

Add all the ingredients to a shaker filled with ice, shake, and strain into a frosted martini glass with a nutmeg rim.

black bison

2 oz. Zubrowka vodka

¼ oz. Chambord
(or crème de mure)

½ oz. fresh lime juice

a dash of simple syrup

4 black currants
(or blueberries)

one blueberry,
to garnish

The central ingredient in this mix is Zubrowka, a vodka that tastes of freshly cut hay, and lends a distinct quality to any cocktail. Combine this with Chambord (a black raspberry liqueur from France's Loire Valley), and you have a truly memorable union!

Muddle the fruit in a shaker. Add the remaining ingredients to the shaker with ice, shake sharply, and strain, into a frosted martini glass. Garnish with a blueberry.

cheesecake

a graham cracker
2 teaspoons simple syrup
2 oz. vodka
½ oz. Chambord
½ oz. raspberry purée
½ oz. heavy cream

You'll need a spoon with this one—it's effectively an alcoholic dessert.

Grind the cookie into crumbs, add the syrup, mix, and pack everything into the bottom of a martini glass. Add the remaining ingredients in to a shaker, shake and strain gently over the crumbs into the martini glass.

turkish chocolate martini

I've always wanted to find a credible drink that includes rose-flower water, and here it is. The heaviness of the crème de cacao combines with the lightness of the flower water to create a truly Turkish delight!

Add all the ingredients to a shaker filled with ice, shake, and strain into a frosted martini glass with a cocoa rim.

2 oz. vodka

¼ oz. crème de cacao (light)

2 dashes of rose-flower water

cocoa powder (for the rim)

lemon meringue

2 oz. Cytryonowka vodka
½ oz. lemon juice
½ oz. Drambuie Cream
a dash of simple syrup

When set the challenge to create something special with Drambuie Cream, I thought I'd bend the rules a little. Mixing citrus fruits with cream liqueurs generally isn't recommended for cocktails, but somehow this concoction resists the temptation to curdle.

Add all the ingredients to a shaker filled with ice, shake sharply, and strain into a frosted martini glass.

herbed + spiced

Creating herbed and spiced martinis requires a little extra effort, but prepared with proper care and attention, these cocktails will bless the drinker with that timeless quality of the classic martini. While infusing vodka may overlap in some people's minds with buying preflavored vodka, remember that the person doing the infusing (that's you) holds all the cards. If you are creating chile vodka with habañero chiles, it is your decision to maim or merely incite! Place the bottle in a cool environment to infuse in a refined and delicate manner, or for a quicker, more brutal method of infusion, the liquid should be left somewhere warmer.

raison d'être

Who says "twisted" martinis are a modern phenomenon? This cocktail originated from a Parisian jazz club called Aerobleu in the late '40s.

2 oz. Russian vodka

a dash of vermouth

6 raisins

a sprig of rosemary, to garnish

Stir the vodka and the vermouth with the rosemary in a mixing glass filled with ice. Strain into a pre-chilled martini glass over 6 sliced raisins and garnish with a rosemary sprig.

hibiscus

It's always worth experimenting with the Hibiscus before you serve it to your guests, as the concentration of the juice can vary—overdo the hibiscus if in doubt.

1 oz. vodka

a dash of lime juice

a dash of framboise liqueur

2 oz. hibiscus cordial*

2 cups sugar

¼ pound hibiscus flowers

1 quart of water

an hibiscus flower or petal, to garnish

Add all the ingredients to a shaker filled with ice, shake sharply, and strain into a frosted martini glass. Garnish with a hibiscus flower.

*To make the cordial, dissolve the sugar and hibiscus flower into a quart of water on a low heat. Once the liquid turns deep red, strain and leave to cool.

cowboy hoof

Who knows where the name for this minty special originates! The color of the drink alone is worth the effort. Do pay attention when straining the mixture—bits of mint sticking to the teeth is never a good look.

12 mint leaves

2 teaspoons simple syrup

2½ oz. gin

a sprig of mint, to garnish

Shake all the ingredients in a shaker filled with ice and strain into a frosted martini glass. Garnish with a sprig of fresh mint.

lemon grass

A gentle hint of lemon grass is all that is needed for this concoction to work. Try this martini before sitting down to a Thai meal. The lemon grass skirt in the photo is not a recommended garnish (unless you have a diploma in basket weaving.)

Add the vodka to a mixing glass filled with ice, stir until the glass is frosted, and strain into a frosted martini glass. Garnish with a thin slice of lemon grass.

Place two split lemon grass sticks in a bottle of vodka and leave to infuse for two days.

2 oz. lemon grass-infused vodka*

3 sticks of lemon grass (one to garnish)

elderflower

Elderflower cordial has become a must-have on bar shelves in recent years—try this recipe with gin instead of vodka as a base, and marvel as the juniper and other flavorings in the gin combine with the sweet elderflower!

2 oz. vodka

½ oz. lime juice

½ oz. elderflower cordial

a dash of simple syrup

a dash of orange bitters

a lime zest, to garnish

Add all the ingredients to a mixing glass filled with ice, stir until the glass is frosted, and strain into a frosted martini glass. Garnish with a lime zest.

classic cosmopolitan

2 oz. lemon vodka
½ oz. triple sec
½ oz. lime cordial
1 oz. cranberry juice

Sex and the City made this drink popular, its great taste ensured it stayed that way.

Add all the ingredients to a shaker filled with ice, shake sharply, and strain into a frosted martini glass.

ginger cosmopolitan

2 oz. lemon vodka
½ oz. triple sec
½ oz. fresh lime juice
1 oz. cranberry juice
2 thin slices of ginger
burnt orange zest, to garnish

A superb variation on one of the great modern classics. The trick is to get the amount of ginger just right. The mix of flaming orange zest, ginger, lime juice, and lemon vodka gives this drink an incredible depth of taste.

Add all the ingredients to a shaker filled with ice, shake sharply, and strain into a frosted martini glass. Garnish with a flaming orange zest.

cajun

A word of warning, this drink must be monitored while it is infusing. Habañero chiles are among the strongest in the world and should be treated with respect.

Add a large measure of vodka to a mixing glass filled with ice and stir until the glass is frosted. Strain the mixture into a frosted martini glass and garnish with an habañero chile.

* Place three habañero chiles (with seeds) in a bottle of vodka and leave until they start to loose their color (the more translucent they become, the more flavor has been absorbed).

2½ oz. habañero-infused vodka*

4 habañero chiles (one to garnish)

tokyo

This martini can be a bit scary if it is made badly. Try to find the best-quality wasabi and the freshest ginger.

2 oz. gin
2 thin strips of fresh ginger
a small roll of wasabi
ginger strip, to garnish

Add the ingredients to a shaker filled with ice, shake, and strain into a frosted martini glass. Garnish with a thin strip of ginger.

licorice

For a stronger flavor, or if you're in a rush, pop the licorice into a bowl of vodka and place it in a microwave on full power for two minutes. Admittedly, it's not a natural thing to do because it does burn off some of the alcohol, but if you want to cut corners …

2 oz. licorice-infused vodka*
a dash of Pernod
2 strips of licorice (one to garnish)

Pour the vodka into a shaker filled with ice and shake sharply. Rinse a rocks glass with a dash of Pernod and discard the liquor. Fill the glass with ice. Strain the mixture into the glass and garnish with a strip of licorice.

* Add a 4-in. strip of black licorice to a bottle of vodka and leave for half an hour.

red star

Unlike the Licorice Martini, the Red Star is a delicate drink. Make sure the glass is well frosted to highlight the hint of aniseed taken from the seed of this Chinese plant.

2 oz. vodka

½ oz. star anise-infused dry vermouth*

2 star anise (one to garnish)

Add the dry vermouth and the vodka to a mixing glass filled with ice and stir until the glass is frosted. Strain into a frosted martini glass and garnish with a star anise.

* Infuse one star anise in a bottle of vermouth (Noilly Prat) for two days.

pegu

This one was discovered in an old cocktail book and given a new life. Originally made at the Pegu club in Burma c1900.

1½ oz. gin
½ oz. Cointreau
½ oz. fresh lime juice
2 dashes bitters

Muddle 2 fresh lime wedges in a boston shaker. Add rest of ingredients and shake well. Double strain into chilled cocktail glass and garnish with lime twist.

cold cure

Strictly speaking, not a martini, well actually, in no sense of the word, a martini. But why should I deny you the joy of one of these on a technicality.

1 oz. Wray and Nephew rum
¾ oz. runny honey
½ oz. lime juice

Stir the ingredients before adding the ice until they are mixed together. Add ice, shake sharply, and strain into a pre-chilled martini glass.

index

CONVERSION CHART

Measures have been rounded up
or down slightly to make
measuring easier.

Imperial	Metric
½ oz.	12.5 ml
1 oz. (single)	25 ml
2 oz. (double)	50 ml
3 oz.	75 ml
4 oz.	100 ml
5 oz.	125 ml
6 oz.	150 ml
7 oz.	175 ml
8 oz.	200 ml

acknowledgments

A big thank you to all of the team behind the mixologist. Most notably to William Lingwood, his ability to bring drinks to life is second to none. Thanks to Helen Trent, whose enthusiasm is bettered only by her eye for objets d'art. Much appreciation to Alison for excelling in her role as my literary mentor, and thanks also to Miriam and Susan, for putting in all the real hard work. Mostly, thanks to my mum for all the obvious reasons.

The author and publisher would like to thank the following companies and stores who loaned materials for the book: The Conran Shop +44 (0)20 7589 7401; Fandango +44 (0)20 7226 1777; Harvey Nichols +44 (0)20 7201 8584; Heal's +44 (0)20 7636 1666; Pullman Gallery +44 (0)20 7930 9595; Thomas Goode +44 (0)20 7499 2823; and Undercurrents +44 (0)20 7251 1537.